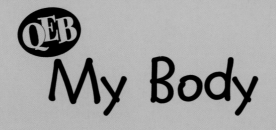

My Body

Why do I sleep?

Angela Royston

QEB Publishing

Copyright © QEB Publishing, Inc. 2009

Published in the United States by
QEB Publishing, Inc.
3 Wrigley, Suite A
Irvine, CA 92618

www.qeb-publishing.com

Library of Congress Cataloging-in-Publication Data

Royston, Angela.
  Why do I sleep? / Angela Royston.
     p. cm. -- (QEB my body)
  Includes index.
  ISBN 978-1-59566-974-2 (hardcover)
  1. Sleep--Juvenile literature. I. Title.
  QP425.R59 2010
  612.8'21--dc22
                                    2009015226

ISBN 978-1-59566-777-9 (paperback)

Printed and bound in China

Author Angela Royston
Consultant Terry Jennings
Project Editor Judith Millidge
Designer and Picture Researcher
          Louise Downey
Illustrator Chris Davidson

Publisher Steve Evans
Creative Director Zeta Davies
Managing Editor Amanda Askew

Picture credits

(t=top, b=bottom, l=left, r=right, c=center, fc=front
cover)
Corbis Brigitte Sporrer/zefa/5t, Randy Faris 8b,
Lisa B 8t, Heide Benser/zefa 9t, G Baden/zefa 14,
Creasource 16b
Getty Images Steve Shott 4, Lonnie Duka 10,
Gala Narezo 16, Tara Moore 17b, Kate Powers 20
Shutterstock Shantell photographe 6, Losevsky
Pavel 7b, Monkey Business Images 9b, Alusinya 11b,
D Barton 11t, Juriah Mosin 12, Gladskikh Tatiana
13b, Zastol`skiy Victor Leonidovich 15, Gelpi 15t,
Tatiana Mironenko 17t, Rebecca Abell 18t, Gelpi
18t, Leah-Anne Thompson 19b, Gelpi 21t, Karen
Struthers 21b

Words in **bold** are explained
in the glossary on page 22.

Contents

Why do you sleep? 4

What happens when you sleep? 6

Dreams 8

A good night's sleep 10

Getting ready for bed 12

Waking up at night 14

Too little sleep 16

Sleeping during the day 18

Resting and relaxing 20

Glossary 22

Notes for parents and teachers 23

Index 24

Why do you sleep?

You sleep because you get tired. Sleeping rests your body, especially your muscles.

When you are really tired, your eyes want to close.

If you sleep well, you wake up feeling refreshed and full of energy.

4

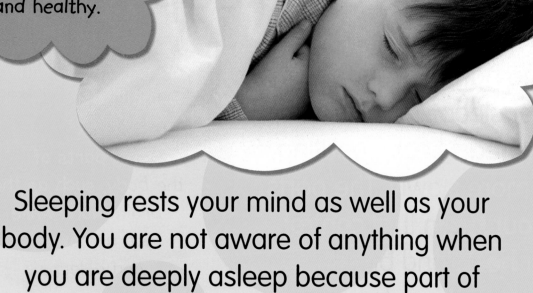

Children need plenty of sleep to keep them fit and healthy.

Sleeping rests your mind as well as your body. You are not aware of anything when you are deeply asleep because part of your brain is resting, too.

Monday 7:30 a.m.
Woke up by myself

Tuesday 7:40 a.m.
Woken up by Mom

Wednesday 7:30 a.m.
Woken up by Mom

Thursday 7:30 a.m.
Woke up by myself

Activity

If you sleep well, you should wake up easily in the morning. Keep a diary to show whether or not you woke up by yourself.

What happens when you sleep?

Some parts of your body never sleep. For example, your **heart** keeps beating, but more slowly. The parts of your **brain** that control your heart and breathing go on working, too.

Some parts of the body, such as the brain, work while you are awake and asleep.

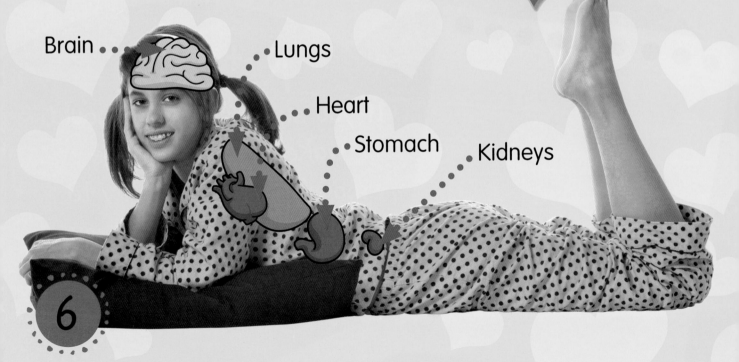

Brain ...... Lungs

Heart

Stomach ...... Kidneys

Your sleep changes during the night. At first, you sleep deeply. In the early morning, you sleep lightly and have **dreams**.

This graph shows how long you might spend in different kinds of sleep.

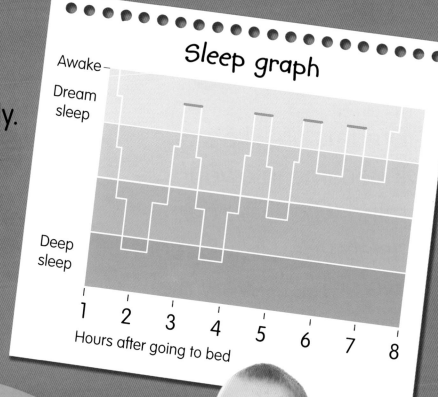

Sleep graph

Awake

Dream sleep

Deep sleep

1 2 3 4 5 6 7 8

Hours after going to bed

Activity

Sit cross-legged with your hands on your knees. Shut your eyes and breathe in and out slowly. Don't think of anything except your breathing. This will calm your mind and slow down your heartbeat.

7

Dreams

Dreams are like stories that come into your mind when you are asleep. You have about five dreams every night. You are most likely to remember a dream if you wake up in the middle of it.

Some dreams are about impossible things, such as flying.

Dreams are often muddled and strange. They help your mind to sort out and remember things. Some dreams are nice, but bad dreams can be scary.

If you have a bad dream, remember that dreams are not real, and they stop once you have woken up.

Activity

Think of a dream that you remember. Tell your friends about it. Then listen to your friends' dreams.

9

A good night's sleep

Most children should sleep for about 10 or 11 hours every night. Children need more sleep than adults because their minds and bodies are still growing.

You are most likely to sleep well if your bedroom is quiet and dark.

You should go to bed and get up at about the same time each day. Your brain then gets used to falling asleep at that time. Make sure your bed is comfortable and not full of toys.

Activity

Keep a diary for a week of the times you go to bed and get up. How long did you sleep each night?

Getting ready for bed

Follow the same **routine** every night when you get ready for bed. This will help you to relax and fall asleep quicker.

Before you go to bed, you should wash your hands and face, and clean your teeth.

12

Avoid playing computer games or watching television before you go to bed. They do not relax your mind. Listening to a story or to music will help you go to sleep.

Listening to a story is a soothing way to fall asleep.

Activity

When you are ready to fall asleep, relax your body bit by bit. Start with your feet. Then relax your legs, followed by your stomach, arms, hands, and face.

13

Waking up at night

Some children wake up in the night
and find it hard to go back to sleep.
You may wake up because you need
to go to the toilet or because
you feel a bit thirsty.

Hugging a
favorite toy may
help you to
fall asleep.

You can help to stop yourself from waking up. If you have a cough, keep a drink of water by your bed. If you wake up to go to the toilet, drink less before you go to bed.

A sip of water can help to stop a tickly cough.

Activity

If you find it difficult to fall asleep, think of something you like for each letter of the alphabet. If that does not work, try counting or doing sums!

$$5 + 5 = 10$$
$$6 - 5 = 1$$
$$7 + 5 = 12$$

Too little sleep

Sleep rests your mind. If you do not get enough sleep at night, you will feel tired during the day. You may be more grumpy, too.

When you are tired, you often yawn. This tells you that it's time to get some sleep.

16

It is harder for your brain to work well when you are tired. You may work more slowly or make lots of mistakes.

If you are tired at school, it will be more difficult to remember what you learn.

Activity

If you find it hard to go to sleep, try having a warm drink, such as hot chocolate or camomile tea. Do not drink too much though!

Sleeping during the day

Babies usually fall asleep at the same time each day.

Babies and toddlers sleep for part of the day. They need more sleep because they are growing so quickly. Older people get tired more quickly and so they sometimes sleep during the day, too.

18

If you get enough sleep at night, you should not need to sleep during the day—unless you are ill. Sleeping helps your body to fight illness and get better more quickly.

When you are ill, sleep can help you to recover.

Activity

Some people say that yawning is catching. Test this idea by yawning loudly in front of other people. Do they start to yawn, too?

Resting and relaxing

Although you should not usually need to sleep during the day, it is often a good idea to rest or **relax**. A rest helps your body recover after rushing around or exercising.

Resting helps you to get your breath back after exercise.

Activity

Some foods may help you get to sleep. Before you get ready for bed, try drinking a glass of milk or eating a banana. Do you sleep better?

After working hard at school, relax for a while and give your mind a rest. You could play a quiet game, watch television, look at a book, or listen to music.

Doing a jigsaw is quiet and relaxing.

Glossary

Brain
Your brain is inside your head and controls every part of your body. Most of the brain goes on working when you are asleep, but the part that makes you aware of what is happening around you "switches off."

Dreams
You have dreams as you sleep. You see, feel, and hear things that seem to be real, but are not actually happening. When you dream, your eyes flicker, even though your eyelids are shut.

Heart
The part of your body that pumps blood to your lungs and around your body. Your heart is in your chest. Your heart beats more slowly when you are asleep. It beats fastest when you are most active.

Relax
When you relax, you rest and become calmer. You relax your body when you rest your muscles. You relax your mind when you do something quiet and soothing.

Routine
A routine is a regular way of doing the same things every day at the same time.

Notes for parents and teachers

1. Talk to your child about how their body and mind needs to rest and recover at night. Sleeping helps them to be energetic and alert during the day. It also helps their bodies to fight off germs.

2. Look for signs that a child may be short of sleep. Are they often tired during the day, or do they find it difficult to concentrate? Children vary in the amount of sleep they need, but most children aged 6 to 9 years should sleep for about 10 hours a night.

3. If your child is not getting enough sleep, talk about what time they should go to bed to give them enough sleep before they have to wake up. Try to keep to this time every night.

4. Set up a bedtime routine that your child enjoys. It could include a bubble bath, a drink of hot chocolate, reading a story, or looking at a book together.

5. If a child often wakes up at night, or has many bad dreams, try to find out what might be disturbing them. Talk to them about dreams and how they are not real. Have fun making up dreams together, in which absurd and impossible things happen.

6. Talk about nocturnal animals that sleep during the day. Have fun finding out about bats and owls that hunt at night.

Index

babies 18
bedtime 11, 12, 13
brain 5, 6, 10, 17, 22
breathing 6, 7, 22

children 5, 10

daytime sleep 18, 19
deep sleep 5, 7
dreams 7, 8–9, 22

falling asleep 10, 12, 13, 14

getting up 11
growing 10, 18

heartbeat 6, 7, 22

light sleep 7
lungs 6, 22

mind 5, 8, 9, 10, 13, 16, 21, 22
muscles 4, 22

relaxing 4, 5, 12, 13, 16, 20, 21, 22
remembering 8, 9, 17
resting 4, 5, 12, 13, 16, 20–21, 22

sleeping enough 16, 17, 19
sleeping in the day 18, 19

tiredness 4, 16, 17

waking at night 14, 15
waking up 4, 5, 8, 14, 15

yawning 19